A... Delight

By Simon Walkling

By Simon Walkling

Cover design by Jane Taylor

Published by:
National Christian Education Council
1020 Bristol Road
Selly Oak
Birmingham
B29 6LB

British Cataloguing-in-Publication Data:
A catalogue record for this book is available from the British
Library.

ISBN 0-7197-0952-0
First published 1999
© 1999 Simon Walkling

Typeset by National Christian Education Council
Printed by Henry Ling Limited, Dorchester, Dorset, DT1 1HD

Contents

Introduction

It's easy to slip into talking about the 'real' meaning of Christmas, as if the other things we get wrapped up in are not part of the celebrations. When I was little, the tree and TV and cards were part of the real Christmas. As a teenager, family tensions were really part of Christmas. Now, as a parent, I'm delighted that our young children can take as much pleasure in singing about the baby Jesus as they can in opening presents. If we try and separate the 'real' religious Christmas from the rest of it, I am not sure that we will really be celebrating God coming to the bustle and bureaucracy of the world.

This book of sketches started with the Scouts and Guides connected with our church wanting to have a Christmas celebration. Lessons and carols did not seem appropriate with the age range, but they needed material that could be practised on their meeting nights, which were at different times during the week. It is difficult to find published sketches which only involve one gender, so I started writing. The results have been used in church and the local high school, and can be adapted to a variety of settings.

The Angels, The Shepherds, Women at the Inn and *The Kings* are a reflective look back, using some of the knowledge we have now. *Christmas Cards, The Generation Game* and *The Free Gift* look at different aspects of Christmas today, to see whether they reveal anything of the good news of Jesus' birth. *The Fairy on the Christmas Tree* suggests that sacred and secular needn't be separate when we are remembering that God was born in Jesus. With each sketch are 'starter points' which could be developed in a short talk or discussion.

Hopefully, these sketches might start some searching and, while angels delight to praise God above, they may help us move closer to true adoration.

Simon Walkling, January 1999

The Angels

This sketch begins from the fact that the angels in the Christmas story often have to say, 'Don't be afraid'. It goes on to think about our pictures of angels, and the fact that angels are God's messengers.

Starter Points

✳ Does modernizing our methods change the message?

✳ How do we react to the challenge to change that is part of the message?

✳ How do we think of angels (literally, 'messengers')?

Cast, Props and Setting

3 people;
a fashionable set of clothes;
a harp cut out of cardboard.

The angels should be dressed in some kind of identifiable uniform that is relevant to the audience. Examples could be Guide or Scout uniform, school uniform, choir cassocks and surplices, or whatever sportswear or football strip is in fashion.

The angels walk on humming 'Hark the herald angels sing'.

Angel 1:   It's always the same. I seem to scare people half to death. As soon as I've said, 'Hello', I need to say, 'Don't be afraid'.

Angel 2:   I know. As soon as we appear they try and hide behind the nearest curtain, or chair, or sheep.

Angel 3:   You don't think it's the way we're dressed, do you? Do we look frightening?

Angel 2:   I don't know ... perhaps we need a new image.

The Angels

Angel 3:   Yeah, perhaps if God's got some spare time, he could sort us out a new uniform. And if he can't do it, we could ask Vivienne Westwood.

Angel 1:   That would scare people even more. I've always found the traditional look very serviceable. *(Continuing in the voice of a fashion correspondent)* The harsh light of the titanium white tunic is balanced nicely by the fluffy feathery wings.

Angel 2:   Besides, we do need something that doesn't burn up when we break into earth space-time.

Angel 3:   *(Giving a sideways look to number 2)* That's as may be, but wouldn't something a bit more up to date be less intimidating? *(Puts a little black dress and a pair of Doctor Martens, or equivalent, on the table)*

Angel 1:   But we need something that won't fade in the wash.

Angel 2:   Or bobble with frequent wearing.

Angel 1:   Perhaps it's our musical accompaniment? Perhaps it puts people off? *(Puts cardboard harp on the table)*

Angel 3:   *(Excitedly)* That's it! We need guitars and synthesizers instead of harps and trumpets!

Angel 2:   Nothing wrong with harps! — What do they say, 'the music of heaven to play with the language of heaven...'?

Angel 3:   Yes, but we're messengers, we shouldn't let anything get in the way of getting our message over. It is good news of great joy for everyone!

Angel 1:   She's right, God has sent his chosen one to save the world.

Angel 2:   *(Reflectively)* Mmmm... Glory to God in highest heaven, peace on earth and goodwill to humanity... Do you think it's the message that's the problem?

Angel 3:   What, that it's not us but the message that scares people?

Angel 1:   That God comes close?

Angel 2:   That God wants things to change?

Angel 3:   That Jesus links God and humanity?

Angel 1:   But that's Good News!

Angel 2:   Yeah, but it puts the wind up me.

                (Walk off in silence or lights go down)

Women at the Inn

This is a sketch about the other people who were in the inn, whilst Mary was giving birth in the stable.

Starter Points

❋ What was Bethlehem like, with all the bureaucratic busy-ness?

❋ What breaks down barriers between people? Sharing in unusual situations? Sharing reactions to common human experiences?

❋ What is salvation?

Cast, Props and Setting

3 females:

Martha   – *whose husband is the innkeeper;*

Hannah   – *a local from Bethlehem;*

Mrs Cohen – *a 'nouveau riche' lady from Jerusalem, who married into a rich family, but grew up in the countryside. Her posh exterior and manner cover humble beginnings.*

The scene is set in an inn, with a table like a bar, and a bell to ring for service.

Martha has a teatowel and an apron.

Hannah holds an empty glass, which she either holds to her, or waves around when she is making a point.

Mrs Cohen has a bag, which she holds in front of her, as if for protection.

Costumes could reflect the period, or be modern dress reflecting the relative social positions.

Scene opens with Hannah leaning on the bar with a glass. The interruptions need to be timed well, or it might be better to make up suitable ends for the sentences.

Hannah: What do you have to do to be served round here? It's all very well opening up to all and sundry from far and wide, Martha — but what about us locals? We keep you in lip gloss all year round!

Martha enters with a teatowel, polishing a glass.

Martha: Now, now, Hannah, you haven't been waiting that long. We *are* running an inn here, we're supposed to put people up. But the census means that the town's over-run with visitors.

Mrs Cohen enters and rings a bell on the table.

Mrs Cohen: Excuse me, my good woman! I was led to expect a room with a veranda overlooking the town square. Instead, we look down into the stable yard, and when we leaned out the window the smell was awful.

Martha: I'm very sorry, Madam, that was the last room available. If you had been able to book ahead...

Mrs Cohen: *(Interrupting)* My husband comes from a priestly family, his father was a member of the ruling council: we did not expect to *need* to book!

Martha: All I can do is apologize, madam. It's the census. I've just had to put a couple in the stable that you're complaining about, because there's no rooms anywhere. *(Turning to Hannah)* She's only a young thing and she's expecting. She's huge, I should say it's nearly time.

Hannah: *(Pointing at Mrs Cohen)* That's the thing with this poll tax — no respecter of persons or situations! *(To Martha in softer tones)* Has she had to come far?

Martha: Nazareth, I think, I better just pop and see what's going on. *(Leaves)*

Women at the Inn

Mrs Cohen: *(Posh accent slipping)* I remember when Josiah was born. I moved to Jerusalem when I married Zadok. Mum couldn't leave the farm when the time came, and Zadok was serving in the temple *(Posh accent returning for a moment)* — a very important job, you know. *(Country accent back)* But I felt so small and alone with only the maid there.

Hannah: When our James was born I nearly screamed the house down, and then with our Sarah...

Mrs Cohen: *(Interrupting, but not rudely)* Yes, yes, but afterwards it's worth it.

Martha: *(Coming in excitedly)* It's on its way! I'm just popping out for the midwife — Rachel Asaph was a great help to me when my three were born, and she hasn't lost her touch. *(Leaves)*

Hannah: I don't know what all the fuss is about. Children are nothing but trouble and worry. They wake you up in the night when they're little, they keep you up waiting at night when they're courting, and they keep you awake worrying when they're married. *(Shakes her head and makes some kind of local exclamation — 'What are they like?', 'Oi vey!', or similar)*

Mrs Cohen: Josiah has always been a comfort and great company for me. I'm only sorry I couldn't have more.

Martha: *(Bursting in)* It's a boy!

Hannah: Have they got a name?

Martha: The girl says his name will be 'Jesus'.

Mrs Cohen: That's a nice name — 'God saves' — that's what it means — that's nice.

Hannah: I wish God would save. It'd get these Romans out of our hair for a start. *(Makes to spit over her shoulder)*

10

Mrs Cohen: Now, now. Roman investment has been very constructive for our economy, Zadok says. There's more to salvation than politics.

Hannah: Oh yeah –

Martha: *(Interrupting)* I want no arguments about politics and religion in here, I run a peaceful inn, I do.

Mrs Cohen: *(Looking out of the window)* There's people coming into the yard. They're looking for something.

Hannah: That's all we need — it's them shepherds. Hang on to your handbags, girls, they're a lot of thieving –

Martha: *(Interrupting again)* Hannah! Look, they're going into the stable.

Hannah: *(Going over to look as well)* Shepherds! They think they're rugged — big outdoor types, coming down here seeing what they can scrounge, who they can–

Martha: *(Interrupting yet again)* Hannah, will you watch your language when we've got nice company? They're coming out.

Mrs Cohen: Look, he's got a great big smile!

Martha: And that one's got tears in his eyes! Who'd have thought it! It must be a very special baby.

Mrs Cohen: Oh, can we see him too — I love babies!

Hannah: Let's all go.

(All leave)

The Shepherds

This sketch involves three of the shepherds that heard the angels' message, and hurried to find Jesus. They talk as if they are looking back from now.

Starter Points

✳ How are the stories passed on to us?

✳ What is special and what is ordinary?

✳ What is holy and what is secular? How does the holiness of Jesus compare to the holiness of the angels?

Cast, Props and Setting

3 people.

Costume can be minimal, or towels on heads to give a suggestion, or fuller nativity-play-style shepherd dress.

Caps, anoraks and wellies could be an alternative.

A number of people somewhere are singing the first verse of 'While shepherds watched'; half of them should be singing the alternative:

>While shepherds washed their socks by night
>
>All watching BBC,
>
>The angel of the Lord came down
>
>And switched to ITV.

Otherwise the shepherds themselves could walk on singing the first verse of 'While shepherds watched' followed by the alternative.

Shepherd 1: They're singing our song again.

Shepherd 2: It's amazing that, all these years on, they're still singing about us. I mean, we were only ordinary people.

Shepherd 3: I want to know how they knew about the socks —
it's not like our washing is interesting.

Shepherd 1: That's oral tradition, that is. Things stick in
people's minds. Stories get passed on. We told
people what we saw, they told other people. The
mother who stored it all up in her heart — she
told someone else... And so on, till someone wrote
it down, and other people copied it, then it got
printed, then put on floppy disk and CD ROM...

Shepherd 3: *(Interrupting)* I wish I'd never asked!

Shepherd 2: Even so, we were just ordinary people, minding our
own business...

Shepherd 3: *(Interrupting)* And our sheep.

Shepherd 1: Yes, ordinary shepherds minding our sheep, but
what we saw wasn't ordinary. Those angels!
(Excitedly) The music filled the air and our ears, and
our hearts!

Shepherd 2: Yeah, it was mind-blowing. It was before fireworks,
and laser shows, and B-Sky-B. Before telephones,
and space flight, and video wall satellite links.
Seeing all that was unexpected, scary...

Shepherd 1: *(In a respectful loud whisper)* Awesome.

Shepherd 2: Extraordinary.

Shepherd 3: *(Looking at the other two)* Yeah, yeah. OK. But the
stable was ordinary. With animals and hay
and stuff.

Shepherd 2: *(Wistful in remembering)* In the cold night you could
see the animals' breath in the lantern light.

Shepherd 3: And a baby. That was ordinary, people have babies
all the time.

Shepherd 1: *(Reflecting)* Those quick little breaths as he slept.
And then when she unwrapped him to change
him, those little fingers: perfect in miniature.

Shepherd 3: And that cry!

The Shepherds

Shepherd 1: But don t you see? That's it ... the ordinary became special. The promise and potential for life and love in every baby, became the hope for eternal life in God's love in that baby.

Shepherd 2: Ordinary life became special, because he shared in it.

Shepherd 3: Ordinary blokes like us became special because we were there, and willing to go and look.

Shepherd 1: That's what Jesus does — makes the ordinary special — that's what 'holy' means, that is — the ordinary being special.

Shepherd 2: So it's a shame when the special becomes ordinary.

Shepherd 1: When tinsel and turkey become a chore.

Shepherd 2: When paper and parcels mean more than the love that gives them.

Shepherd 3: When the special wonder of God in everyday life gets lost in Christmas musak.

Together: We wish you a holy and happy Christmas.

The Kings

This sketch is similar in idea to *The Shepherds*. It is a conversation amongst the wise men, as though they were alive now, reflecting on their journey then. The wise men's careful study and committed journey are a contrast to the shepherds' direct technicolor vision.

Starter Points

❋ How did the wise men work? Why did they go to Herod?

❋ Can we see any significance in the gifts they brought?

❋ Do we need to search to understand Christmas? Or does it depend where we begin from?

Cast, Props, and Setting

3 males.

Appropriate costumes could be used to convey a traditional picture of three kings.

A group sings 'We three kings of orient are', and some sing the alternative, or the wise men themselves sing the original and then the playground version.

'We three kings of orient are	'We three kings of orient are
bearing gifts we traverse afar	one in a taxi, one in a car,
field and fountain	one on a scooter
moor and mountain,	blowing his hooter
following yonder star.'	following yonder star.'

King 1: Young people today ... they don't know how hard it was.

King 2: I wish we had had a car or a taxi, it would have been easier on the backside than those camels.

The Kings

King 3:   *(Rocking backwards and forwards)* That journey made me realize why a camel is called the ship of the desert — it's because they make you seasick!

King 2:   Have you heard the latest though, about the possibility of life on Mars?

King 1:   Yes, in our day it was Mars in Saturn rising meant a good harvest, now it's all space probes and computer analysis.

King 3:   All we needed was a few charts, a good eye, and a pair of compasses. My teacher always used to say, 'A clear night, a clear head, and make sure you're well read.'

King 2:   That's true. If you hadn't read those Hebrew prophets, we might never have made the connection that night we saw the new star.

King 3:   I'll never forget that star... *(Looking into the distance, looking into the past)* The way it twinkled... its royal beauty...

King 1:   It's a shame you didn't get as far as the bit in the prophets where it mentioned Bethlehem, then we could have avoided Herod the horrible.

King 3:   *(Defensively)* You were the one that said a king should be born in a palace. *(Starry-eyed again)* I remember the way the star *moved*. One expects seasonal variation, but that star drew us — led us on, right to the place where we found Jesus.

King 2:   I know, we hardly had time to get presents. Then what we did take wasn't that appropriate. We would have been better giving a babygrow and a travel cot.

King 1:   Well, I thought gold was a *good* choice: a sound investment. More secure than shares in the long run, and without the danger of negative equity you get with property. And later on he could have had some nice pieces of jewellery made.

King 3: I remember I'd just done that aromatherapy course, and they said that frankincense was very relaxing for new mothers, and soothing for babies with colic.

King 2: I had terrible trouble getting that myrrh. Delia Smith had put it in one of her recipes, with cranberries and elderflower cordial.

King 3: Considering all that, it's amazing how appropriate they were.

King 1: Yes. Gold for a king — for the one who is king of the universe with God, and rules in the hearts of those who love him.

King 3: Frankincense for a priest — for the one who showed us what God is like, and made a way for us to be close to God.

King 2: And myrrh used in preparing bodies for burial – for the one who made this possible by dying and bringing new life.

King 1: *(Tired now)* Yes, the first journey was hard. But the journey to understand it has been harder.

King 3: We gave expensive presents to Jesus, and he gave costly love to us.

Christmas Cards

In this sketch characters from the Christmas cards look down from the mantelpiece and talk about what they can see. The robin and the coachman are trying to make sense of the tree and Christmas TV, and the Snowman tries to be intellectual. The shepherds come as an unwanted intrusion at the end to remind everyone about Jesus.

Starter Points

✳	How can we use the Christmas trappings to convey something of the good news of Jesus?

✳	What is important to people at Christmas?

✳	Does what we do show what is important to us, or how we think about it? If someone was watching us, what would they think was important about Christmas?

Cast, Props and Setting

5 people.

The characters can be indicated by what they are wearing (or costumes can be as elaborate as ability allows):

A Robin — red waistcoat or jumper
A Coachman — cape and whip or posthorn
A Snowman — hat and scarf
Two Shepherds — teatowels on heads

The title of the sketch needs to be emphasized in the introduction so that the audience or congregation know that the characters are from Christmas cards. It may be good to perform this sketch from the side of the hall, or the gallery of a church, to get the idea of the cards looking down on the living room. However, making sure that the sketch can be heard is the most important thing.

Robin: I'm a robin on a Christmas card
My red breast stands out bold.
Though there's a smile upon my beak
My tail feathers are cold.

Coachman: I'm the driver of the mail coach
Bringing a Christmas greeting,
My hands are stiff and my feet are cold
Because it won't stop sleeting.

Snowman: I'm the snowman on a Christmas card
It's a bit warm for me in here,
So turn the heating down a notch,
And bring me an ice-cold beer.

Shepherds: We're the shepherds on the hillside,
The religious card in the box,
The 'who on earth can we send this one to?'
The shepherds abiding with flocks.

Coachman: So, cock, what do you make of this Christmas business?

Robin: I like the tree. It's a nice rural touch. Makes me feel quite at home.

Snowman: Rural touch! *(Exasperated)* Rural touch!! That's evergreen, that is. That's your hope when everything else is dead and dormant. That's light in darkness, that is: a reminder of Light and Life!

Robin: Well, I think it's nice.

Coachman: That's not what *She* says when she's hoovering up the needles.

Robin: OK, you asked the question: what do you think of Christmas?

Coachman: I've been watching that tele-box in the corner. It seems to me that Christmas is a re-run of past Christmases, and about arguing what to watch.

Robin: I can't decide whether it's the tele-box thing that causes the arguments or that buttons thing that

	they point at it. Either they can't find it, or they're arguing over it.
Snowman:	I don't believe it. Christmas TV is a highlight of the season! Everyone loves to complain about it, and arguing about it takes the steam out of other arguments.
Coachman:	It's all repeats of Christmas Specials!
Snowman:	Go on! Laughter brings people together, and repeats are part of your secular ritual, remembering the past to give energy for the future.
Robin:	Do what? Part of what?
Snowman:	Oh yes. I may be here today, gone tomorrow, melting into the mists of memory, but I knows you know.
Coachman:	It's only because they show 'The Snowman' every year on Channel 4. Go on then, you overgrown ice pop — what do you think Christmas is all about?
Snowman:	'Sobvious, innit? Easy as A, B, C. A is for advent calendars. B is for boxes. C is for cards. D is for drink. E is for evergreens. F is for family, food, and friends!
Shepherd 1:	*(Who has been silent and still till now)* And G is for God who came to earth, H is for humble which was his birth.
Shepherd 2:	And I for Immanuel, a name which means 'God with us' and the reason for the season is J, which is Jesus.
Robin, Coachman and Snowman:	Who invited them? *(They walk off one way)*
Shepherds:	The angels, actually. *(They walk off the other way)*

Free Gifts

Sometimes during the year we talk about Christians failing to harness modern techniques and opportunities to get the good news across. At Christmas we often feel that the good news is hijacked by commercialism. This is a sketch which asks us to question how we would feel about the kind of promotional campaign modern culture might produce.

Starter Points

✳   What makes an impact on children?

✳   What is the Millennium about?

✳   What is the real 'free gift' of Christmas? God's love!

Cast, Props, and Setting

4 people;
Minimal props and costume.

The scene is a meeting of executives of a fast food chain, trying to decide what toys should be given with children's meals in 1999. There is the Boss and 3 executives. The first two keep trying to get the Boss's attention with tried and tested ideas. The third is getting more excited as she sees the whole scheme coming together.

The fictional fast food chain and characters could easily be changed to reflect the restaurants in your area.

Start by singing 'MacDonalds, MacDonalds, Kentucky Fried Chicken and a Pizza Hut.' Don't worry if you don't know this!

Boss: Welcome, everyone. I'm Wilamena MacFryit the Third. I want to open this meeting of the Burger Hut Free Gift Forward Planning Strategy Action Group. Our agenda today is to decide what gifts

will be given out with kids' meals in the weeks
leading up to the new millennium.

Executive 1: That's the end of 1999, right?

Boss: Right.

Executive 2: Kinda new beginning thing, right?

Boss: Right.

Executive 3: It'll be Christmas just before.

The others: So?

Executive 3: Well, we could have wind-up shepherds. You could have a group of shepherds in the middle of some sheep, and when you wind it up, the sheep run round the outside.

Boss: *(Bemused)* We've not had anything like that before.

Executive 1: Christmas, yes! We can have a little plastic Burger-man dressed up as Santa Claus.

Executive 2: And Milkshake-girl dressed up as the fairy on top of the Christmas tree.

Boss: Would they do anything?

Executive 3: *(Excitedly)* You could have angels that flap their wings when you move a lever at the back.

Boss: *(Bemused again)* Angels?

Executive 2: Or we could do something from the latest film. They usually shift the stuff well, kids always want the latest merchandise.

Executive 3: *(Inspired)* Kings! We could have kings as well. Three varieties: a clockwork king on a camel; a king with a box that really opens with a yellow plastic gold brick inside; and a kneeling king that bows its head in worship!

Executive 2: Or we could do Skinny doll. Skinny goes down well — Skinny skating; Skinny sledging...

Boss: But what about the boys, what about the international dimension — it's not snowy at Christmas everywhere.

Executive 3: Right, I've got it now. 1999, four weeks leading up to Christmas... In the first week we give Mary sitting on a donkey, led by Joseph. Second week we give shepherds. Third angels. Fourth three wise men. The box is the same each week, it comes apart to give backgrounds of hills and sand dunes, and the other bit unfolds to make a stable. Then, then in Christmas week, we give the baby lying in a manger.

Executive 2: *(Scoffing)* A manger? A baby!?

Executive 1: What's that got to do with the season to be jolly?

Executive 2: What's it got to do with the millennium?

Boss: *(Interested)* Explain.

Executive 3: It's simple. Christmas celebrates the birth of Jesus, the Son of God born as a baby in a stable in Bethlehem. The millennium will be 2000 years since his birth according to our calendar. Jesus still gives hope and life to millions all round the world.

The other executives look amazed.

Boss: Radical. Fits with our ecological care for the planet and society image. Build up your own crib scene. Let's go with that. Meeting closed.

Executive 1, Executive 2, and Boss walk off. Executive 3 left thinking...

Executive 3: *(To the audience)* It's not too tacky is it? *(Follows the others)*

The Generation Game

A mother, her daughter, and the grandma deal with Christmas.

Starter Points

❋   What causes tension at Christmas?

❋   How do we communicate with those close to us?

❋   Does 'Peace on Earth' translate to peace in our homes?

Cast, Props and Setting

3 females.

The daughter needs to be in a short skirt, the grandma

should have several cardigans or a shawl. Mother could be in

an apron, with her sleeves rolled up.

Together:	'Twas the night before Christmas, and all through the house, there was trouble a-brewing: ALL HELL WAS LET LOOSE.
Mum:	*(Angrily)* I don't care how warm Sam's house is - you're not going out in that skirt!
Daughter:	What's wrong with it? Everyone will be wearing them!
Mum:	If you can't see what's wrong with it, I'm sure I'm not going to tell you!
Grandma:	*(Gently)* It is a bit short, dear. I should think you'll catch your death of cold. You have got a vest on haven't you?
Daughter:	Vest?! I grew out of vests ages ago!

Grandma: (*Shivering*) Don't worry, you'll grow into them again before long. (*Turning to the mum*) And you should put a cardigan on too, I'm cold.

Mum: Aw, Mum! I thought you'd stopped telling me what to wear years ago. (*Turning to her daughter*) Now, my girl, upstairs and change.

Daughter sulks but doesn't move.

Grandma: Do I know this Samantha you're going to see, dear?

Daughter: Samantha?

Mum: Samantha?!! I said she was going to Sam's! That's not Samantha, it's Sam, her boyfriend!

Grandma: (*Shocked*) In a skirt like that?!!

Mum and daughter both make exasperated faces.

Daughter: It's OK, his parents will be there.

Grandma: When I was your age, we all went around in a big group of friends, carol singing and such... And we wrapped up warm.

Mum: (*To daughter, but more friendly*) I thought that you might stay in tonight, and help with the preparations a bit. I like it when we do stuff together.

Grandma: Yes, we could all watch the film. 'The Slipper and the Rose' is on, that would be nice.

Mum and Daughter look at Grandma as if she is from another planet.

Daughter: But I really want to see him tonight. He says he's got a present for me, and I've told him that I can't see him tomorrow, because I like to be with the family on Christmas Day.

Grandma: I love sitting down to Christmas Dinner with everyone, and pulling the crackers, and laughing at the jokes.

Mum: I relish that moment when all the cooking's done and everything is steaming on the table, and no one quite knows where to begin.

The Generation Game

Together: *(But in their own little dream worlds)* Yes, I like a family Christmas.

Daughter: So can I go, now? Please?!

Grandma: Has the heat gone off? It's gone chilly in here.

Mum: *(A little deflated)* Yes.

The three go off in different directions.

The Fairy on the Christmas Tree

This is a monologue growing out of an old song, and thinking about the fact that 'angel' is simply the Greek word for 'messenger'.

Starter Points

❄   How do we think of angels?

❄   How do we cope with things at Christmas not being the way we want them to be?

❄   How do we share the good news with those who say, 'Christmas is a family time', or 'Christmas is really for the children'?

Cast, Props and Setting

1 person. This could be a female, or a male dressed up like a pantomime dame.

The poem is helped by the person wearing a toy tiara, a length of tinsel as a scarf round the neck, and a wand made out of wire coathanger covered in tinsel.

Note that, to give some changes of pace, the meter and rhyming pattern are not the same throughout.

> Every little girlie wants to be
> the fairy on the Christmas tree.
> But I'm the fairy on this year's tree,
> and I want to be an angel — see!?

The Fairy on the Christmas Tree

I was put in a box for safe keeping,
in white tissue layers so soft;
and I knew that Christmas was coming –
it was getting cold in the loft!

Despite all the care that was taken
the past months have not been too kind;
my wand has got broken in transit,
and my tinsel's begun to unwind.

Well:

They straightened my wings out quite nicely,
and my wand is looking quite pert.
So I'm perched on this tree until Twelfth Night
with evergreen stuck up my skirt.

It's not what I'd call a vocation;
an angel's what I want to be:
I may have dreams 'bove my station,
but I want to fly around free.

I want to take tidings to shepherds,
and sing of God's peace on the earth.
Bringing good news to ord'nary people,
spreading joy for the Saviour's birth!

But I'm stuck here for the duration,
while fairy lights blink on and off,
because of my rising frustration
I think I deserve some time off.

I'd swap this tiara of plastic,
and hand in this old tinsel frill,
for a halo of light that's fantastic
and the glow of God's love and goodwill.

I hope that by now my meaning's plain,
and this will be my loud refrain,
when Santa's magic is drowned in rain,
I'll sing of God's good news again

Of Jesus who is God with us —
a miracle that's fabulous.
Of a baby born among the poor,
so we can live for evermore.

Of God who gives meaning and purpose,
by sharing our life here to bless;
whose love makes the best even better,
and stays close in grief and distress.

So whether you're crowded or lonely,
you know we can all play our parts:
It's not just for children and families,
but for all who let God in their hearts.

I stand here just doing my duty,
pointing that Christmas is coming.
I try to rely on my beauty,
and the words of the carols I'm humming.

Then inside a voice whispers gently,
as quiet as a twinkling light:
'You know that "angel" means "messenger",
and it seems to me you're just right!'

So light the candles, and deck the hall,
and dress the tree, but most of all
sing of the babe in the cattle stall.
I am an angel after all.